Lyrical Years

Lyrical Years

Poems by

Gary D. Grossman

Cover design by Shay Culligan
Cover images by Gary D. Grossman

ISBN: 978-1-63980-263-0

Kelsay Books
502 South 1040 East, A-119
American Fork, Utah 84003
Kelsaybooks.com

For Barbara, Rachel and Anna

Acknowledgements

These poems or versions of these poems represent works written over 30 years and published or appearing in:

Athens Parent Magazine: "6:35 AM," "Night Noises," "Anna Age Three and One-Half, Takes an Interest in Fashion," "Reflections on Painting the Kitchen"

Black Poppy Review: "Stealing a Line From Proust," "Sleep"

Blood and Fire Review: "Carnivory," "A Cardinal in January"

Delta Review of Poetry: "Popping Shrimp Heads"

Feh: "Personal Values," "Dancing in January," "Beach Bugs," "Dining on Tybee"

In Your Face: "A Poem"

Last Stanza Poetry Journal: "Budbreak," "Moderation" "Rainbows, Brown, and Brookie," "Figs July 26, 2021"

Lilliput Review: "Athenian Tragedy"

McQueen's Quinterly: "Cherry Bombs"

Medusa's Kitchen: "Cloacal Kiss"

Muddy River Poetry Review: "Pacific Coast Highway One"

Night Roses: "Kudzu in Clarke Country"

Pearl: "I Have Always Wondered"

Poetry Motel Broadsides: "Uncried Tears"

Poetry Superhighway: "Stealing Two Queries From Proust"

Poetry Life and Times: "Unexpected Disturbances" "Rhododendrons Blooming in the Smokies"

The Acorn: "While Clouds Linger Over Dreams"

The Knot: "Poetry on the Listserve," "The Minute I Realized I Was Old," "On Getting a Tattoo," "Jetlag," "Cleaning Out My Office After Four Decades"

Trouvaille Review: "Chalk," "Hummingbirds at the Feeder in August," "American Sycamore"

Truck: "Rolodex," "Chimney Swifts in Athens, Georgia"

Contents

Learning the Ropes

A Second Walk

Maturity Is an Aging Wine

Novicehood

Personal Values

About twenty years ago,
I had a girlfriend in LA,
who became my first love,
though not the woman
I have loved the most.

We did all the first love things,
the moist loins thing,
the lying to parents overnight trip thing,
the matching rings thing,
the everlasting devotion thing,
the break up every 6 months
sleep with someone else then
get back together again thing.

When I moved to Berkeley for school,
everlasting devotion stayed in LA.
She was 17
but promised to move up
18th birthday morning.

Then her parents told her
they would take away
her car and horse,
so she didn't.

Which put the first crack
in my heart, though I did learn
my worth as a person,
which was less than the cost of
a 3-year-old roan gelding,
and a '68 VW in good condition.
But it didn't bother me all that much,
'cause things were
a lot more expensive then.

Pacific Coast Highway One

Mill Valley fog
lies down, with the
practiced ease of a
former lover,

whose supple limbs
enfold again,
creating problems
for me and my
new wife.

Sleep

isn't easy, the white slap
of fear hits just when I glide
from dusk into night.

I was 12, Mom unwakable,
pills strewn across furrowed
sheets, black buds amidst the dunes.

Now, falling asleep has the
coppery taste of oncoming
headlights, closing in my lane.

I flinch,

and . . .

Jet Lag

Turbulence forgotten,
my neurons still fire,
flicked by the digits
of two skim lattes.

Excitation and
exhaustion hover
sleep's ebony arms
just off my chest.

While my thoughts careen,
cottontail before
coyote, through sage
and eucalyptus,

to bring me to the dawn.

A Poem

Just showered
water sparkles on
the creamy canvas
of your skin.

You lean over the bed,
correcting the sheet.

My gaze traces
the contours of your hips,
ripe with promise.

You hear my impending touch,
voice edged in laughter, you say
"don't you tickle me," and
when I giggle, add,

"and don't write a poem about it,
either."

Uncried Tears

Lying on
the sterile draped table,
I smiled as I saw you
in a black and white world.
"Just a check-up," the OB said,
"a precaution."

Unknowing,
I watched your reflection
slide from the doctor's face,
his eyes like French doors,
slamming shut, then reopening.
He said, "There is a problem."

And staring at
the grey-filled screen,
I wondered,
had you already met
your older sister and brother,
somewhere,
in the house where tears are made?

I Have Always Wondered

why
pregnant women snore
so much.

Awakened at two am
by shaking walls,
while she still sleeps.

But surely it's exhausting,
to share your air and blood
with someone else.

Apostrophe

Where are you now, my sons,
my daughters? Swept from Mom's

womb for cause, no pulsing
heart, no movement. Nothing

left to say, as once again
your mere milligrams

crush my eyelids, halting
salty streams. I was sure

my heart beat strongly
enough to hold us all.

But the roll came up
snake-eyes, and you are

now just a shadowy
gray sonogram bean.

My jaws clench when
someone outside the

hospital asks "How ya doin'?"
But I am silent, rain

falling from my thin
chestnut hair on to my shirt,

forgotten hat in hand.

6:35 Saturday Morning

In bed, we sit,
backs supported
by grandmother's
Ukrainian pillows,
a wedding gift.

Coffee steams,
bitter as a
moonless winter night
tamed with milky
clouds.
You sip formula.

Our ages
38, 2, 40: the code
to a filigreed lock,
warding braided lives.

Daylight parts
slatted blinds,
dust fairies dance,
and our quilt is striped
with gold and umber.

Reflections on Painting the Kitchen

Two kids,
two cars,
careers.
Too much,
sometimes.

I wanted poplar green, but you held fast.
Now when the sun crowns
the corrugated fields above our home
it coats the room with streams of amber,
can't shake 'em loose, won't slide off.
I let their belly-warm glow
seal my every jangling corner.
So though I doubted yellow,
with your help I've learned
the kindness of the color.

Carpal Tunnel Syndrome

Hands punching decades on keyboards, and
an old IBM Selectric. On even days
my fingers tremble and on odds
numbness holds their pruney tips.
"Occupational hazard," they
say. The Muse has her price.

Shaking a brainy head, my Doc
states "Not yet" to surgery, and
assigns homework telling me, "Find a
strong rubber band, insert fingertips,
then force them open, over and
over again." My own tiny pulsar.

On a whim, I discover the
perfect band secures the weekly
bouquet, that I bring my beloved.
In spring, budded pink roses,
tangerine lilies in summer, ruby
mums in fall, and winter is potluck.

Lagniappe, these rubber circles. White
or purple, width barely half an
inch, surprisingly tensile. I
insert five bussing fingertips in
the band, expanding and contracting,
my hand now a dancing crab.

Every night, I make the crab plie
30 times, and it is working. My
hands now stable as Rodin's
aptly named "Cathedral," a 1908
bronze of two lightly triangled
hands. This, a sculptor's affliction too.

Such linkage—writing, to compressed
nerves, to roses, to rubber bands
to physical therapy, and back
to stronger hands. Look closely—
the world is more connected
than it seems.

Flotsam & Jetsam

Flotsam,
an accident,
cans loosed by
twenty-foot combers,
climb and fall,
climb and fall,
bow skidding
into the trough.
Keys, wallet,
lines, adrift,
unleashed by a
chance slip.

Jetsam,
debris heaved
for cause,
life lightened.
Entanglements cut free.
Remora friends
and eight-armed guilt,
drift to a cobalt gyre.
Baggage to lose,
so years are
not an itchy wake.

Stealing a Line From Proust

The silver-haired man on my
right asked "Where and when were

you happiest?" "Right here, right
Now," I replied, beckoning

the barmaid to bring us both beers,
while sweat ran down the gutter

of my forearm in this Ensenada
cantina, ablaze with cumin

and ajo. I smiled and gazed
across a Tarot of compadres,

plenty of cups, but no swords or
wands, unless you're a magician,

amigo, or a physicist.
Both manipulate the

ether and its bodies of
unseen flammable forms.

Happiness is doing what you
want, when you want to, and

that is the why, here and now
of this beer, tangible hops,

malt, and rime-glazed mug.

A Walk Outside

Chimney Swifts in Athens, Georgia

                              As dusk unleashes
                    the ebony bones of night,
            sleek chimney swifts
                              slide home
                to roost.
    Chittering
                gusts of
                    black confetti,
                                    they flutter,
                        falling,
                into the
                sleeping
                stacks
                of the red
                brick mill,
                that fed
                our town.

31

Dancing in January

This morning I was startled
by the listless ice crystals
splayed in sparkling embrace
on the windshield of my truck.

They had tangoed through the dawn.

Cherry Bombs

Such small worlds,
one inch—maybe two—
red as a tiny Mars
or yellow; a flaring sun.

My taste buds explode,
tartness painting a
startled tongue, fleshy
pulp, sour and sweet

rides an umami wave
plunging down my throat.
I am eating summer,
offspring of a green

boned vine. Luscious orbs,
popping, until my stomach
gurgles no more—no
more—no more tomatoes.

Cloacal Kiss

Mid-February and the red-tails
and red-shoulders dance across
the sky, shouting *ki-ah, ki-ah*
birdtalk for "look at me, look at me."
A pick-up bar in a cerulean
sky, with raptors circling and
chanting "hey baby, hey baby."
Mating is a cloacal kiss
an uninspired and rapid
act of amour—white bread sex—
Butts touching for just a few
seconds, male on the female's back
bending downwards uniting his
cloaca with hers, and the next
generation begins.

Cloaca, ancestral orifice,
a single opening for genital
and excretory pores. Birds, fish,
snakes and amphibians.

Which reminds me of the old adage
that our bodies must have been designed
by engineers, because only an
engineer would have put the sewage
treatment plant, adjacent to the
amusement park.

Carnivory

In the piney flatwoods,
where colors hide
from August's heat,
I found them,

gathered along
a graveled road,
in soil, rich as
chocolate soup:
pitcher plants.

More than
two hundred,
leafy soldiers
standing pat,
silent in ambush,

awaiting the
next nosy fly.
Vainglorious, and
juicy fat.

A Cardinal in January

Like an ember,
feathered crimson
with a blush
from the sun's dark eyes,

he perches
on a snow-clad limb,
contesting snowflakes.

Like a hearth-warm ember,
gently unfolding
the bleached hands
of winter,

he brings life
to crystalline January,
like the red breath of embers,
or the shadowed flare
of his murmuring flight.

Church of Georgia Route 17

Turkey buzzards
gather in roadside
pews, releasing
the souls of
dead possums
and squirrels.

Figs July 26, 2021

Last spring's rain pounded
the earth—riverine flows
danced over iron-red
soil.

While hydrangeas chanted
praises. And mild temps
made lily and asters
saunter upwards.

July slid in, and the
fig tree was cloaked in scent
like a bottle of Joy perfume
left unstoppered.

The palmate leaves hummed, and
quickly assembled hundreds
of purple-dressed fruit, they
dropped off sticky stems.

Pods of living jam, they were
too sweet, too many—small orbs
of candy flesh splitting skins
two sizes too small,

like jeans bought at 18
I too have ripened.

Snake Handlers

Not a preacher from
some Appalachian holler
not a carny or a zoo tech.

I'm a vertebrate ecologist
teaching a small seminar
for new uni students.

Mostly I dispense fact-
snacks through the virtual
slots of graphical software,

but today, is herp day—
Live reptiles and amphibians
come to class for study.

Students are mostly from burgs
ruled by concrete or lawn. Full
of their 18 years, wearing

the current fads, gym short and
long tees, fancy running shoes
that rarely achieve peak speed.

Only a rare one has held live
frog or turtle let alone snake.
The girls are the bravest,

perhaps more committed to
the proposition that
toads aren't scary.

Modern Eves, unfazed by
the snake and apple and
the lie of original sin,

they coax one another with
mild jibes among friends,
but as afternoon closes,

most have held the three-foot
lengths of Corny, the corn snake.
or Lady, the king snake.

Not mere touches, but minutes
of close contact. Learning
to support their slithering frames.

"Don't grab, just let them flow"
across forearms and biceps, over
open hands and flushed warm skin.

A life lesson, one hopes, historic
selfies and the closing words
"That, was cool."

Kudzu Is the Real Thing

Kudzu has no morals,
not polite,
no blushing begonia,

not helpful,
like aloe,
or mint,

not aromatic,
like jasmine,
or honeysuckle,

no ambiance,
like Virginia creeper
or dogwood.

Hell no, kudzu's
an in your face
plant.

A get out of my
way or I'll bury
you, plant.

An "I came to this
country, did just fine
on my own" plant.

So keep a good watch,
always be wary
with kudzu around
even chlorophyll's scary.

Cicadas, Brood X

Seventeen years is
a long wait, though
love cuts the years.
The roots of wild asters
were succulent in
year eight, as were the
water oaks in 12,
and maple rootlets
in year 15, *ooh la la*!
Dark memories, the
many tastes on my rostrum
sweet, sour, and the
umami of
day lily tubers.

I was sitting on a poplar
branch, tymbals buzzing
when you landed.
Eyes glowing like
rubies from Ceylon,
and such shapely legs,
three pairs of jointed,
stilts, all intact, not a
single one missing.
Golden-veined wings like
a Tiffany window
from January 1908.
My heart pulsed in
need. And your wings
clicked *"yes, to say
yes . . ."* as we coupled
to make Brood XI.

Learning the Ropes

Unexpected Disturbances

Damn, what the hell?
I shuffle upstream, rod
in hand, just outside the
rhododendron line, and
I'm struck by flying needles
forearm, ankle and neck.
Effing yellow jackets.

Mother drove poorly
always fiddling,
cigarettes or radio,
until her '65
Karmann Ghia vaulted
a 30-foot embankment
on the road cleaving

the sage-shrouded hills
between Tecate and
Tijuana—DOA
This story is true, not
artistic license. I
was orphaned at eighteen,
no sibs, no dad.

And so life is an
erupting Krakatoa,
a Hurricane Katrina,
an unexpected disturbance,
COVID-19, recession
cancer, bipolarity
and yellow jackets,

until the chips are cashed.

Babe Ruth Struck Out 1,330 Times

Who remembers that?

Walt Disney,
fired from the
Kansas City Star
"lack of imagination."

Stephen King's
Carrie, was rejected
30 plus times. Now a
best seller.

Richard Nixon's
political career,
over in '62.
Okay, bad example.

Holding my 86th
rejection letter,
I repeat, "Babe Ruth
struck out 1,330 times."

Night Noises

toilet,
faucet,
refrigerator,
squeaking limbs,
slap of the cat door,
whippoorwill's chant,
dust raining onto dresser tops,
warm air tickling heating vents,
moon light skidding down louvered blinds,
an edged plea skidding round the bedroom door,
"Daddy, I'm scared, please come sleep in my room."

Anna, Age Three and One-Half, Takes an Interest in Fashion

Your puckered mouth
indents my thigh,
an artist's brush
glides back and forth,
and down and up,
as more of lunch
is nuzzled clean,
upon my pants.

Now blotched
with amber,
edged in red,
the leavings of
a ripened peach,
a chartreuse stripe
from spinach too.

My wardrobe heralds
new couture,
designed with patterns
from your plate,
those cheek-print shirts
match lip-blotched pants.

A millennial parent, PhD,
I'm a four-foot napkin,
neck to knee.

The Dishwasher

1.
Rearranging the dish-
washer is my "thing."

A family joke run amok,
I peer over shoulders,

"Dad, aren't you glad we're
even putting plates in?"

But I move two blue-striped
bowls from bottom to top

and the small plates to the
center, unblocking the

rotating sprayer. Wife
and daughters laughing,

"Does it really matter?"
And of course it doesn't.

Like so many things done,
and said every day. Force

of habit or the mirage of
control of our environment,

as in this is "my" house.

2.
It is my one attempt at
Engineering—or is it Geometry?

Filling a finite space to
to the maximum. Efficiency

squared. Or you might just
think me lazy. While I

ensure the lowest number
of dishes that I myself must

wash. Or perhaps a mild
neurosis, my inability

to just let things slide, like
lights on throughout the night,

accepting what I cannot change.

3.
When they were younger
and had friends sleep

over, after lights out, when
they were nestled in bed

small bird voices would
fly out from their

slightly opened doors.
"What's that noise?"

"Oh don't worry, it's
just my dad rearranging

the dishwasher."

Hand Sanitizer

Years, no, weeks ago,
I had no use for hand
disinfectant.

No peering at a label's
alcohol content, like
I do for bottles of
Cabernet.

Or wipes. I mean
who carried those
around—cleansing
store entrance knobs
and just purchased
Ho Hos?

Should I buy
a clear bottle
or a tinted one?
Should I wear a mask?
May I touch my face,
or my wife's, or
my daughter's rosy cheeks?

So many questions.

These Are My Gifts

For the wedding of Rachel and Nauroze

These are my gifts to you little bird,
grown yet growing, young yet old,
wise yet learning,

these are my gifts.

Not sculpture nor jewels,
not peaches nor perfume.

My gifts to you are the wind and rain
and the forest and seas.

My gifts to you are freedom,
tolerance, and an open heart.

So when he eats the last slice of pizza,
drinks the last can of soda,

he will you know.

And when he's always late
remember my gifts.

The freedom to grow into yourselves,
the tolerance of best friends,
the love of hearts growing whole—

these are my gifts.

Stealing Two Queries From Proust

Run finished and exhalations
fogging the 43-degree air,
I stood by the island-like green
park bench, while the spread-eagled

undergrad with torn leather shoes,
said, "I'm doing a philosophy
paper and I need to know—when do you
feel justified in lying?"

I replied, "Such strange words,
laying and lying, frankly,
I get them confused. One a
simple rest the other falsehood.

That's the truth. Lying or is it laying?
Similar yet different. But you
are a stranger and I should sleep.
That's a lie—so the when is now."

Which reminded me of the time
my son asked, "How would you like to
die?" I answered, "Asleep, laying in
my bed on satin sheets. No lie."

The Losses of COVID-19

They ask, "What do I miss most?"
A tight hug, I say, more than
fifteen seconds. The warmth of
bodies, known and new. The softness
of blouses, and even the crushed
goose down feeling of insulated
coats. Memories freed by someone's
scent. Hugs, coming and going,
greeting and parting, new or
familiar. Hands lightly stroking
my back, granting a good squeeze.

Chalk

I found a used piece of chalk in
the mustard yellow-green box
tucked in the bottom drawer, of
my walnut office desk. It was chilly
as a northern wind, and slick as
a rainy windshield. Rolling it back
and forth between my fingers I
remembered the power of circles.
The rollers that move blocks of granite.
Our arteries circulating blood at
such high pressure. Tree trunks pulling
life from soil and crumpled leaves.

A shape without corners hides nothing
and surprises everyone.

Moderation

1.
Flew home from Israel,
in week two of the Plague,
fourteen-day quarantine,
and my Zayde's haint,
rasps, "Idle hands . . . Devil's friend."
So I'm painting our mange-
blotched, 1940s Cape Cod,
our peeling, white, heart-haven.

Kibbutz Mizra, Plague day four,
I flail against the government's web.
Cancelled flights and shuttered stores.
in the Holy Land,
where the air rustles nervously,
despite greening hills. And
there is no moderation.

The new order tells
my hotel to shed me,
like winter fur in April.
But kindness prevails,
and I remain, fed even.
Anxiety forecast now
cloudy with occasional sun.

2.
Plague safety and painting
are best taken in moderation.
Six feet apart outside but talk,
sixteen feet up the ladder,
but please, no farther.

Mental health jogging but
personal distance from step one,
rules too harsh, you rush,
overload the brush—

paint drips and spatters
on finished spaces.
And the virus persists.

Painting is meditation.
Smooth, silky brushes,
caress the clapboard.
Our house-skin now
sports layers of ivory.

3.
Life and painting—both
ninety percent preparation.
Wash, scrape, prime;
mask, wipe, scrub;
listen, think, act.
Zayde said, "Anything
worth doing, is
worth doing right."

But I know I'll always have
spots to touch-up.

Transformation

Avocados follow
the laws of physics.
Not conservation
of mass, but Newton's
Third—every action an
equal and opposite
reaction. And the
Second law of
thermodynamics,
because this avocado,
grocery stacked yesterday
like green cordwood, and at
least as hard, has become
entropic overnight, now
a flaccid globe of
canary and brown flesh.

Such a transmutation—
how and where? In the tan
paper sack perched on
the rear seat? No—still
firm exiting the bag.
In my kitchen—secretly
caressed at night by
the ethylene Lilith
that seduces all my fruit,
because bananas do
me the same way?
Who knows?

A minute, an hour,
a day, we are all
slowly dissolving,
fodder for the next star.

A Second Walk

Cabin Fever

Annoyed with February,
I flung open the door,

to a landscape awhirl
with confectioner's sugar.

Physics is wrong,
I found two alike.

Rainbow, Brown and Brookie

A mélange of rubies, emeralds,
and opals, they slide through
a cold riffle, holding where
the insects drift downstream;
easy prey, just a quick snap.

Years stretch like too-old elastic,
and I have tired of them, baked, or
wine-poached, sautéed in yellow
butter, decades of slick plates and
twisted skeletons, fleshless on
the communal bone-china plate.
The scent of scales and crisp
skin wafting into the dining room
from our sun-colored kitchen.

So I bought a smoker.

That left their flesh amber, yet
firm, apricot-tinged, flinty, and
dry as Sancerre in July.

Every one I catch, I swear,
"The next one will go free."

While Clouds Linger Over Dreams

Redbuds awaken early
from the starched night of winter.

Blossoms sliding upward,
through gray sheets of sleeping bark.

Radiant,
like newly-forged suns,

they speed the breath
of the stubborn trunks of March.

Kudzu in Clarke County

Conquers old Fords,
shacks, unwary pines.

Sinewy tendrils
push leaves

green as a
lover's darkest thoughts,

snaring us with
twirls and purple blooms,

Till December's
solid air,

sweeps her to a bed
of rusty clay.

American Sycamore

It is a ghostly obelisk of a tree,
breathless among the paused
leafless gray soldiers of the forest.
Post and water oaks, shagbark
and mockernut hickories, red- and
chalk-bark maples, and silverbells.
So many trees hold up the cobalt
southern sky.

White on white echoes through
the Georgia woods in January
and the visual music pulls my eyes
back to the solitary sycamore, trunk
shedding a few last puzzle pieces
of elderly taupe bark.

Forty-nine years ago I met the
companion who now walks beside
me on the trail—today we are
the wrinkled, white-barked, trees
of the town.

Beach Bugs

Sand gnats
go splat,
against my arm,
against my hat.

You are too fat,
oh cunning gnat,
with blood from this,
and blood from that.

Hummingbirds at the Feeder in August

The dwarf flyers dogfight,
emerald backs edging
to buff, figure eights and
double barrel rolls,
all for a refueling perch

on the tanks of pink
sugar water held by the
scarlet and yellow-petaled
falsehoods hanging from our
small grey-green side porch. The

birds rage over these ten
square feet, like Liston or Ali,
who floated like a butterfly
but couldn't hover like a
hummer. Backstroking, they

float, folding the air into
neat sheet-like stacks, blackened
tails flared in anger and
accusation. They surge back
and forth like erratic feathered

pendulums until
one jet cedes the air but
two more shoot from holly
twigs, a tornado of
enraged plumage, jade

cream and onyx, resembling
nothing so much as a
perpetual motion
machine composed of wings
feet and bills. I slowly

crack the kitchen/porch
door, avoiding impalement
by the mini-jet roosting
in my neighbor's magnolia.
So far, just near misses,

jet wash brushing my face, I
jerk backwards, a human slinky.
The birds are irate sentinels,
chiding all who near their
liquid hoard. Tssst, tssst, tssst.

The sun arcs southwards and
instinct rises. Tank up
for Belize, 26,300,000
body lengths away, then
back again, when dogwoods

bloom and April's leafy
smells entreat. The feeder
will be up, runway lights
glowing green. All systems
go.

Beech Trees Dancing in Winter

Fifty-two days of grey skies
and not even a bath in my
"nature light" can strip the
dark film from my skin.

So I begin walking through air so
thick its frozen scent has fallen
onto the oak leafed soil, and
end up at the local woods.

Here the copper beeches dance, arms
branched and strong enough to hold
their latte-colored leaves through
the muscular angst of February.

They are ballerinas with
silver tights and ginger hair,
subjects for Degas had he
walked these Southern woods.

I can't help but smile.

Dining on Tybee Island

I saw a trail
made by a snail
in the middle
of the mud.

I asked him, "Why?"
His answer, wry,
"I eat this crud."

Rhododendrons Blooming in the Smokies

In Summer's rumpled heat, the blue
scent of hemlocks slides upwards,
spreading comfort across the ridgetops.

Stooped shoulders the ridges, remainders
of pinnacles, scoured by centuries
then slowly cloaked in maple and oak.

Just below the ridgetops, an emerald
sea, sharp pines weaving winds
that unfurl through the hollers.

From the top of a ridge I can almost
touch them, reach down through wet air,
to green-bedded pink blossoms.

The fluttering hearts of a slow-rolling valley.

Maturity Is an Aging Wine

Budbreak

For JW and WW

1.
March 22, and life pivots,
Mother sun climbs the rungs
of her annual ladder,
solstice to equinox.
In the Georgia woods,
a lone wren calls.

Ground fog rises
through trunks etched
in grays, and corrugated
browns. The aged
palettes of Bruegel,
Elder and Younger.

But small greens call
spring's name, that
boisterous child of
each solar cycle.
Trees leafing out
fast as snapped fingers.

Mint, moss, and shamrock.
Limbs put on lime
cloaks and ripen
to olive, like my
skin, aged from
ivory to speckled tan.

2.
Leaf-fall is months away,
and that final winter.

Three score and ten, yet
not for all. Wyatt, 21,
who dove again, and again,
into a chemical sea.

Arms extended, we
reached through
funneled currents, and
wrestled the ten-armed
reaper, but the
boy surfaced no more.

3.
Kids grow up, old
friendships crack, like
greenstick fractures.
Reunions of convenience,
neighborhood shops,
and the local pool.

At the memorial,
she broke when I held her.
Salty rain on my shoulder,
and a burden, like
Lot's wife. Surely I
could have done more.

But the buds will
break again next year,
and the next, woods
bursting green; late March
or perhaps early April.

Rolodex

Mossy dust covers
the black plastic case.
Time buries some things
faster than others

A dead solar system,
cards rotating around
the now-dark axis
of my Rolodex.

It sits tilted in the trash—
born before recycling.
Where are my colleagues
now, floating somewhere
in the digital vapor?

In electric cirrus or altostratus,
new guardians of data?
Or is it cumulonimbus,
with gigabyte drops,
waiting to be clicked,

engulfed by the cloud?

The Minute I Realized I Was Old

came when smoothing out
wrinkles from the prior life
of a twelve by fifteen inch
rectangle of aluminum
foil. Now a small metallic
square reflecting our
lemon-painted kitchen,
I bury it in the wrapper
drawer, where it will
discuss reincarnation
with its plastic cousins.

On Getting a Tattoo

1.
I'm not sure when
I actually knew my
own mind.

Opinions stable and
straight as hundred-year
white oaks.

Experience the key,
choosing door one instead
of three.

Living abroad,
learning a foreign
tongue.

How can nouns
have sex? How can
they not?

Our differences all loop
back to shared red
heme.

2.
The old joke, "Marriage
sure, but a tattoo is
permanent."

Faded black-green
text on 35-year-old
skin.

How will it read
when the decades
sag?

So not yet. Arms
uninked. Thirties pass, and
forties bring

two blond girls.
Dad—a good example
be.

"If you get one,
they will too." So,
not yet.

Years unfurl, now
college kids. Example?
Quien sabe?

Raised right, no
parental fetters.
Now.

3.
Example be damned,
decade seven is mine,
left forearm

interior now inked. A
heart built of breaking
waves.

Cobalt fading to pearl,
ringed by Barbara, Rachel,
and Anna.

A permanent reminder—life
flings us to and fro. But strong
arms are there to catch us.

Popping Shrimp Heads

Five pounds of white shrimp,
fresh off the Anna Jane,

Tybee Island, Georgia.
chitin-wrapped gifts from the

cordgrass haven where Bull
and Savannah Rivers embrace

to form the Atlantic Ocean.
The shrimp are a satiny

translucence. A string of soft
marine opals, eyes now glassy

black beads peering up from
our stainless-steel sink. Each

hand holds a shrimp, as the green
olive scents of Spartina and

pregnant mud scuttle upwards.
Grasping bodies gently, I

turn them, pleopod legs
to the outside, avoiding

polysaccharide lances,
that exact revenge for

lost crustacean lives, but
the sticks are inevitable,

because this is barehanded
work, gloves unable to palpate

the springy crevice between
thorax and abdomen where

a thumb must enter and with
Guillotine flick, separate

the transparent rectangle of
head, guts and antennal whips

from sensual tail-meat. The
head tumbles downward joining

the decapitations of other
noble crustacean, laying on

the sink's silver floor. Steam
rises from Gramma's dented

black stockpot. Scents of bay, mustard
seed, coriander, and cayenne.

The boiling water
jitterbugs in anticipation.

Thanksgiving Recipe Poem 2021

Ingredients

1 Partner
1 Child 4–6 years of age
1 Child 8–10 years of age
1 Set of Parents
1 Set of In-laws
1 Brother, spouse, and two teenage boys
1 Uncle Bob between 72 and 75
2 Cases of Mixed Five-Year Old French Bordeaux and Spanish
     Riojas, both white and red
Usual Foods—turkey, sweet potatoes, broccoli, lettuce, cranberries

Seasonings

1 Set of Comments About Republican Obstructionism
1 Set of Rejoinder Comments About Incompetent Liberals
1 Set of Comments from Older Relative and In-Laws Regarding
     Child-Rearing
2 Glasses of Wine Beyond the Capacity of Every Adult
2 Questions Regarding the Purchase of European Rather Than
     American Wines
2 Days of Parents Wandering Around House Clucking Tongues and
     Shaking Heads
Endless Patience
2-Day Supply of "I'm Sorry You're Having Such Trouble"

Instructions

Begin preparations on Wednesday before the Holiday, as relatives straggle in three hours late—hungry and tired from traffic. Universal opinion is that tail-gating, speeding and failure to use turn signals is the new normal. Discuss whether Uncle Bob should still be driving, while he is listening. Admonish kids to be on best behavior and not run around the house. Install porn-block on all computers to prevent surprises from teen-aged nephews. Argue about the football game to watch and why the Braves didn't deserve to win the World Series. Discuss which pies can be cooked the day before and agree on pumpkin and apple. Parents begin wandering around house with furrowed brows. Begin two days of "I'm sorry you're having such trouble."

Make quick run to store with brother and sister-in-law, get caught in traffic, only to find tart apples for pie are sold out, as is canned pumpkin. Discuss whether fresh pumpkin will work for pie but decide against purchase. Leave with bottle of "Eat Crow" bourbon and argue over who should pay. Sister-in-law graciously reminds you that you've recently been laid off, and that they offered to host the dinner this year. While bagging the lone bottle of bourbon, grocery bagger asks for some "Thanksgiving generosity" with palm outstretched and pouting lower lip. Fumble for single dollar bill, present to bagger, and receive scowl in response.

Continue drinking bourbon neat. Bottles of five-year-old red Chateau du Grava, Chateau Laffitte Laujac and Marques de Riscal are opened and drunk.

Next Day

In-laws arise at 6 AM and begin watching yesterday's rebroadcasts on the Fox News Channel. With their hearing deficiency, volume projects through entire house, waking everyone except Uncle Bob. Your kids, who have given up their bedrooms for guests, are both in your bed, and begin, along with your partner, to cry. Older teen-aged nephew begins to wander through house displaying Uncle Bob's dentures in water glass to everyone awake. Younger nephew declares he is vegan and will not eat anything.

Everyone is awake. and food preparation begins after heated discussion regarding whether to have breakfast at home or to go out. No one calls the restaurant before leaving and it is closed until the following Monday. The three-car convoy returns home, coffee is quickly made, and blood pressures and pulses slowly return to normal. Uncle Bob has forgotten essential medicine which results in a 1.5-hour drive in traffic, to his home and back. Discussions over food continue, especially regarding when the 22lb turkey should go in the oven. Parents continue wandering around house with worried expression, open various closed doors and issuing occasional "clucks." Brussel sprout side dish is vetoed by acclimation. Kids eat bag of marshmallows meant for sweet potato dish. Turkey is placed in oven at 10 AM, basted with a sherry-lemon sauce enhanced with ground cloves, cardamom, allspice, smoked paprika, and cumin. Highball glasses of Eat Crow resume at 11:30 AM. Turkey cooks for five hours without basting because everyone already is plastered. Basting resumes as does vegetable and salad prep. Turkey is turned breast down to retain juices. Turkey is removed from oven after an additional hour of cooking. Brother and Father-in-law argue over who carves the turkey best. Discussion ends with them agreeing to disagree, and you begin to carve turkey. Inner breast meat is reddish-pink and obviously uncooked. Discussion ensues over the health hazards of eating undercooked poultry. Bottles of white Graves and Bodegas Muga are opened and glasses poured. Turkey is quartered and each quarter is basted and placed in microwave for 12 minutes on high. Turkey fat heats and paints inside of microwave with grease which ignites in minute ten. Turkey is removed and carved into ragged piles of flesh and plated on slightly chipped stoneware platter. In-laws ask if chipped platter is a health hazard because of potential retention of old juices. Broccoli is cooked and seasoned with butter and garlic powder. Top falls off the old jar of garlic powder and half jar goes on the broccoli. Broccoli is rinsed in warm water and replated. Homemade cranberry sauce is bitter, and you substitute canned jellied cranberry sauce left over from last year's

Thanksgiving. Green salad is prepared and dressed with a Dijon-mustard tarragon vinaigrette.

Meal is plated, wine glasses refilled and meal served. Toasts are made to various deceased family members on both side of the family.

Repeat in 2024.

Poetry on the Listserve

The email read, "But how is this a poem?"
referring to my love child, the weekly
poetry post on our neighborhood
Listserve.

"It has no real imagery, no metaphors, just
prose broken up into clauses"—all of this
after sending him the link to *What Is
Poetry*.

He was right of course, and I paused to
look outside and watch the winter sky
peel off its blue jeans and put on salmon
pajamas

I replied, "I suppose a poem is anything
the author and just one reader agree upon."

Voice Lessons

for SC

How are they born, the
universal truths of pitch,
tone, resonance, texture?
To sing like the small wind
painting my lover's skin,
orange-gold tones emerging
like adult monarchs from
chrysalises.

We begin with vocalises,
fantasy syllables to
loosen tongue, palette
and sound box. Eyes
closed, shoulders back,
head centered, leaning
slightly forward on the
balls of my feet, as if
to make a free-throw.

Rectus and transversus
abdominus are
bellows stoking my
vocal forge. Piano
chords ricochet off
studio walls, painted
reassuring green.

The first vocalise,
shu papa, *shu papa*,
shu papa shu hints
at meaning, but instead

just animates the
pine siskins feeding
outside the open
studio window.

The tempo becomes
fierce—too fast—and
eventually my
lips descend into
laughter. We have soared
and stooped through two full
octaves.

More complex vocalises
follow—*ne na nah no*
each note two beats, and
ve o e o e o e o e, and
again, I run two octaves
each, perhaps seven
vocalizes in my
weekly lesson.

Most sessions I vanish
into the notes, nothing
present but vibrating
atoms, speeding from
my lungs.

It is the cleanest
I have ever felt.

Mothers and Daughters Walking

It is June 2020, and my wife
is talking me down, yet again
from the paranoid heights of
imaginary COVID, health
professional that she is. We
quarantine in place, the days
mostly crushed like the
cans in our recycling
bin.

I slide off my harness of fear
by jogging, though my left knee
protests like an unoiled screen
door. So my gait is odd, a mildly
hamstrung horse, for five miles of
therapy.

Who said every cloud has a
silver lining? Surely some are
copper, tin, or even lead. Does
Odin hurl COVID-bolts to keep us
on our toes or do plagues come
from Asgard's random number
generator?

On my jogs during quarantine
I see mothers and daughters
walking. Peas from the same pod.
High school, middle school, even
fourth graders, home for Zoom
instruction, with Mom and
Dad.

Everyone is tired of our ruffled
feathers from months in the human
chicken coop, and we all ache
for the smell of sunlight and
the taste of a fresh breeze. COVID
sent us outside, stretched our legs
at midday, let us relearn how
to listen, even released kindness.

So perhaps there is a silver lining.

My Nightstand Drawer

Slightly ajar, and the diary
of my nighttime needs, or just
things I hold close, a stew of feelings
and wants. Small LCD flashlight
for novels when nightmares rise but
my beloved's inhales and exhales
are regular as summer tides.

White exercise rubber band to
counter five hours daily of keyboard.
Red albuterol inhaler, though
asthma has mostly left the room.
Box of shells for Dad's Remington .45,
that tasted both Iwo and Guadal.

A coarse nail file, so fingertips are
solid on a rosewood fretboard, steel
clippers too. Eight ounces of A&D,
appeasement for skin raw from a
new tat. Four X six-inch notebook and
ballpoint—inspiration at 3:12 AM
stanza and verse.

Half a roll of orange-flavored Tums,
reflux, ugh. The light smell of must,
is it from the minute dust bunny
sleeping in a corner?

Do possessions mark us or are they
void of content? Perhaps a small
autobiography, a material
confession, or just lines on a life
unscrolled?

Going Out to a Movie During COVID

Year two of the plague.
A February evening with
coats and scarves to fend off the
violet cold pack of dusk.

I sport a blue Oxford cloth shirt and
khakis, and you, a slinky emerald
wool dress and heels. For a year our
outer skins have been pajama
bottoms and tees, and it feels as
if we have morphed into the
Snow Moon illuminating
the corners of a colorless night.

Perhaps clothes don't make the man
or woman but I feel as if normality
was slowly repainting my torso.

I reach for the cool brass knob of
the front door, but quickly turn,
draw you close, and say, "Let's kiss
before we leave." A look of surprise,
then your lips part slightly, and our
tongues braid a necklace of linked lives.

You take a tissue from your purse,
and reach up, wiping a streak of
scarlet from the corner of my
mouth, then say,

"I'll have to redo my lipstick."

Athenian Tragedy

Zeno's poetry takes
me only half-
way . . .

The Girl in the Orange Tank Top at Sarah's Creek Campground

Standing by my Volvo wagon,
jeans still shedding the fifty-two
degree river that stole my warmth—

rod in right hand, gut-less rainbow
trout in left, she approached—face brewing
dismay. Burnished copper hair and

skin white as sea foam. Twenty-two,
maybe. River at my back, campground
ahead I had noticed her waving

a cell, freckled arm extended
as she stood on the door ledge
of her red Toyota Solara,

trying to capture a signal wisp.
I suppose the tee was an accent,
an accessory for hair and skin.

But why the stress carving her face?
She drew close and said, "I left my
cash at home and want to camp for

three nights. They don't take cards, and
I can't reach my Mom." Forest Service
intolerance of both plastic

and scofflaws, is well known, so I
asked, "How much do you need?" Clearly
I had been appraised as "a dad,

no threat," dashing my self-image
as an acronym ending in
ILF. I mean, who else but

a dad carries cash "just in case."
She replied, "Thirty dollars, I'll
Venmo you," and I gave her three
tens and a business card and thought,

"The mirror doesn't lie."

Conundrum

I write poetry,
but am I a poet?
When does the title
adhere or the halo accrue?

After twenty-five poems, or
twenty-five publications,
fifty, one hundred? Or success
in *The Atlantic, The
Paris Review*?

Does it require naming?
"My friend the poet"—
and must it be in person,
or COVID-virtually?
Twice or three times?
Who's the scorekeeper?

It can't be monetary.
Who makes a living
via poetry these days?
My best advice to
aspiring poets—don't
give up your day job.

And that MFA,
not sure about that
either, unless you'll
teach and need to meet
"terminal degree in the
field."

Seventy-four publications
later, I'm still asking,
"Am I a poet?"

Finishing Middlemarch

Maybe this will be the year I
finish Middlemarch. One thousand
twenty-six pages, acclaimed the
best novel written in English.
Started so many times I
resemble an engine with fouled
spark plugs, slowly sputtering
along and then dying.

On the first try I got to page
three eighty-two where Mrs. Waule
concludes, "Higher learning interfered
sadly with serious affairs,"
at which point I was so tired of
grading exams that the book
leaped out of my sleeping outstretched
hand, hit the floor running, and was
never to be seen again.

On the second try, I managed
to reach page four forty-seven, where
Will Ladislaw disparages
Edward Casaubon, "And I have
seen since that Mr. Casaubon
does not like anyone to
overlook his work and know
thoroughly what he is doing.
He is too doubtful . . ." Still
unsure why I failed that time.

Then I won a fellowship to
Otago University, in
the home of kiwis, and thought,
"Well I won't be going out
much—a perfect opportunity."

$30 NZ for a used paperback—it
is an island after all. Down
under, I was wrapped in old England
because the South Island,
Dunedin and further South, are as
old England as queuing up and
tea meaning dinner, with the Scots
settling down in Invercargill,
and Hebrides folk on Stewart Island.

But the ghost of failures past floated
across the Pacific and I
only reached page six hundred and one, where
Dorthea Brooke, upon learning
that her deceased husband
Mr. Causaubon, had left no
will, exclaims, "I am quite
well now Uncle, I wish to
exert myself."

Words of inspiration, maybe this
year of COVID quarantine
will do the trick?

Getting Inked at 67

Session One

It is chilly inside and out—Tuesday
in March, everyone masked, but the
repurposed massage table reminds me
that my largest organ, my skin,
will soon serve as canvas rather than
just a tan corporeal container.

The air, a faint wash of spearmint and
isopropanol, as I unpeel my
shirt and lay down, right arm propped
on the black, steri-film wrapped rest. We
agreed on the design, but Keith craves
more skin and complexity. Who,

am I to disagree, an old man
trying to drop the reins and embrace
the universe? Getting inked means
letting go—angst evaporating
like a kettle left too long on the stove.
New image, a helical dragon

complementing the koi ascending
a waterfall on my inner forearm,
replica of Eisen's 1835 color
woodblock. The new tat completes the
origin story of dragons—a school
of koi climbs a waterfall—all but one

murdered by goblins, and at the top
the lone koi evolves, now the Adam
of dragons. Today it's line-work,
black frames to enclose the thick
shades of green, gold and scarlet to come.
Neat lines need a de Sade-like, five-tined

conical needle. Hard-scaled armor, plates,
fins and claws. Arm shaved, stencil applied, and
we're off. Two hours stream by quickly, as I
ignore the low voltage *zzzzzzttt* of
the needle, pain undulating through
bicep and shoulder. I try entering

a trance, but it keeps crumbling like an
old brick wall. Conversation ebbs
and flows, a tide tossing flotsam on a
aural shore. Where were you born?
What part of Athens do you live in?
How long have you been here? There is

no privacy as I lay shirtless. Others appear
on the two remaining tables, in
search of small pink daisies and Celtic
knots—personal pleasures and tightened
love bonds. The undergrads hesitate
to speak, maybe first-timers or perhaps

my lank grey hair. Blood wells on my
arm, and Keith applies witch hazel
and a "glide," A&D ointment to
slow blood seepage and enhance
penetration of ink. The viscous
odors take me back to the shame

of kid's too-wet diapers and
strawberry rash My dragon emerges,
a menacing wraith, black lines tracing
irate skin. Hour four, my muscles twitch
as a spiked worm crawls up my shoulder
then down to my elbow and repeats.

The pain holds a crack-like addiction,
endorphins flowing from nerve cells like
too much rain over red clay soil.
My youngest, now 25, asks if
my intention is to have a "sleeve,"
and an easy "no" escapes my lips.

Session Two

Keith washes the last bit of sausage
biscuit down with milky coffee. Twice
daily coats of A&D salve have
healed my dragon, flaked skin now smooth
and linen-colored. I sit, draping
my right arm over the wrapped, black rest.

I'm wearing a blue cotton running
tank-top to counter antiseptically
low studio temperatures. The
shading needle drinks pine-green ink
from one of seven minipots—pigmented
soldiers standing on parade. Greens—pine

to chartreuse, golds—five to twenty-four
carat, and fiery crimson. *Zzzzzt*
goes the needle, my arm yo-yoing
between pain and acceptance. Shading
less painful but endorphins still flow
and four hours is my exit. Dragon: eighty-two percent

Strangely intimate, this inking business,
as my koi and wave-tossed heart smile.
Unknown bodies working bare skin,
incidental brushes of hands on legs
or breasts on an arm, physical
not sexual. Through the hinged joint of

the Craftsman oak screen shielding the
next table, I see the twenty-something
who's getting a circle of roses
on her left hip. Plague imagery, or
maybe a Grateful Dead fan. She's on
hour three when I leave.

Session three

My dragon still partially naked—fins,
head and belly and pots of ochre,
butterscotch and salmon rest on the
table. A bit of fire for his tongue too.
The chair *eeeks* as I sit and hang my
arm over the rest and wish

for a 5mg Valium like my
kind dentist provides pre-filling.
Not so much for pain but to aid
sitting still four hours. Studio busy,
a sale on small flowers and sorority
girls have descended. But this is my

last session—two and a half hours
later my dragon ready for takeoff.
Ochre head and horns, fiery tongue,
salmon belly, and butterscotch fins.

He glows with power and integrity.
I hope to exceed his expectations.

Cleaning Out My Office After Four Decades

1.
My wife retired last September,
three months emptying her
office that held twenty-five years.
So I multiplied 3 months X

1.6 yielding, "Get your ass
in gear." Now seven months before
departure, I'm in inventory
mode to disperse my academic

detritus, scientific journals,
paper reprints, even binder clips.
My faux oak desk chocked full
of professorial ephemera,

only to find that nobody wants
my shit. Science—relocated
to the metaverse, ones and zeros
the new alphabet, displacing

words on sleek, high-clay paper.
Reprints? What are those? Tears roll
as each glossy article flutters into
the grey recycling bin, and

these leaves from my colleagues'
hearts and minds crumple together.
Many are inscribed "To Gary with
best wishes," and I reflux

a teaspoon of regret while asking
Darwin for absolution. Our kind
custodian has moved the bin
into my office. A green walled,

windowed monk's cell, still retaining
wisps of student's grades and dreams.
But after today's discard session,
only thirty-two years of academic

life remain, books and the small smells
of computer paper and printer ink,
and the thrum of my desktop computer.
Desktop computer? Who owns such

a dinosaur? Today's world is all
about laptops, tablets and smart phones.
Bluetooth reigns, and brain implants are
the next rung on evolution's ladder.

2.
My office is a large living
space, and many times I have
shut the lights, locked the door,
and lay down on the tight curls of

nylon carpet. My eyes close, breath
and pulse ease. Silently, I repeat,
"Hypnosis helps me help myself."
Five reps later my jaws unclench as

I drift, conjuring a boyhood stream
and trout, as the stress-ants emerge
from my muscles, and march out my
feet like SS troopers. My mental

images of inept deans and deluded
colleagues: worn old pieces of
graphite, not diamonds from Tiffany's,
despite their peacock struts in the hall.

3.
My office, my peace island. Sink,
dorm fridge, cans of tinned herring
and smoked trout, a white coffee cup
holds forks and spoons, and rests

next to electric kettle and French
press coffee pot. All will move to the
women's shelter thrift store as will
books on herpetology, animal

behavior and fish population
dynamics. Some will go to my last
two graduate students, strong youths
swimming upstream into the rapid and

complex currents of academe.
teaching, grants and research. The
family photos and award plaques
return home, as will the stained glass

fish hanging in my three windows.
(Recognition brings windows,
plaques, and jealousy.) Each
bejeweled fish represents

a decade of study and enough
published pages to feed both the
ego and front yard winter fire
pit, sitting on iced rye grass.

4.
But is there a mold to recast
my body anew—right arm to
poetry, left to sculpture, legs
to jogging, chest to gardening and

fishing? Forty years—fifty-two
percent of a modern life. My
friends say, "You'll love the freedom,
all your hobbies . . ." They know me well.

But when I still myself and listen
closely, I hear the soft *grrrrrrs*
of the Black Dog just outside my door.

About the Author

Gary Grossman was born in Rochester, NY back in the last century, lived in both Southern and Northern California and currently resides in Athens, Georgia. Now retired, he was Professor of Animal Ecology at University of Georgia from 1981 to 2022. Gary authored or coauthored 150 scientific papers, which have been cited 9,000+ times. Gary's poems have appeared or are forthcoming in 35 reviews, including *Athens Parent Magazine, Verse-Virtual, Poetica, Feh, Poetry Life and Times, Your Daily Poem, Trouvaille Review, MacQueen's Quinterly, Poetry Superhighway, Muddy River Poetry Review, The Knot, Delta Poetry Review, Pearl, Truck,* and *Last Stanza Poetry Review.* Gary was both an essayist and columnist for *American Angler Magazine* from 2007 to 2019 until the zine folded. Short fiction may be found in *MacQueen's Quinterly* and creative nonfiction in *Tamarind Literary Magazine.* Hobbies include running, music, fishing, gardening, and cooking.

Bio and writing at https://www.garygrossman.net and https://garydavidgrossman.medium.com/ respectively.

Made in the USA
Monee, IL
27 November 2023

47478223R10067